Ready Set Sign
Songs for Everyday Transitions

Time to Sign, Inc. | PO Box 33831, Indialantic FL 32940 | P 321.726.9466 | F 321.726.9467

Copyright © 2011 Time to Sign, Inc.

Ready, Set, Sign
Songs for Everyday Transitions

Copyright © 2011 Time to Sign, Inc.

Ready, Set, Sign
Songs for Everyday Transitions

Table of Contents

Songs — Page

1. ABC Song — 4
2. Alphabet Animals — 5
3. Circus Train — 6
4. Clean Up — 11
5. Color Fun — 17
6. Food Pyramid — 24
7. Goodbye — 28
8. Good Morning — 32
9. If You're Happy and You Know It — 36
10. March and Sing — 39
11. Mr. Sun — 41
12. Play Time — 44
13. Rest Time — 49
14. School Bus — 50
15. Traffic Light — 53
16. Twinkle Twinkle Little Star — 55
17. Wake Up — 57
18. What Are We Doing Today? — 59

Handouts

A. Classroom Management Signs — 62
B. Colors — 67
C. Emotions — 68
D. Family & Greetings — 69
E. Manners — 70
F. Numbers — 71
G. Snacks — 72
H. Transportation — 73

Copyright © 2011 Time to Sign, Inc.

Ready, Set, Sign
Songs for Everyday Transitions

ABC's Song

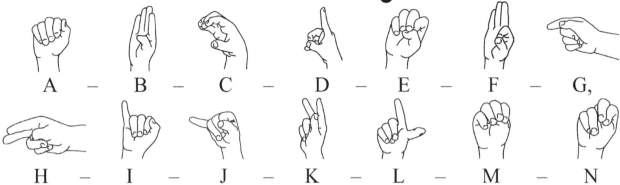

A – B – C – D – E – F – G,
H – I – J – K – L – M – N
O – P,
Q – R – S, T – U – V,
W – X, Y and Z.

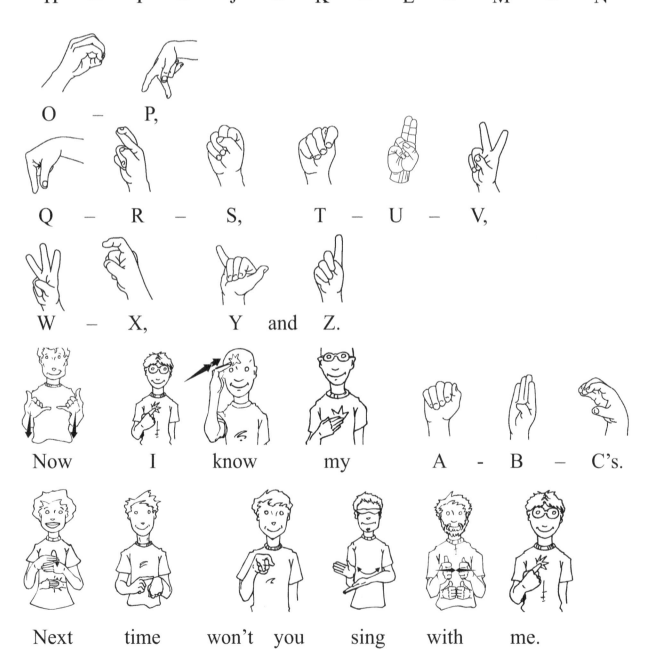

Now I know my A – B – C's.
Next time won't you sing with me.

Copyright © 2011 Time to Sign, Inc.

Ready, Set, Sign
Songs for Everyday Transitions

Ready, Set, Sign
Songs for Everyday Transitions

Circus Train

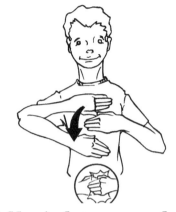  

All right everybody,   all aboard,   get lined up

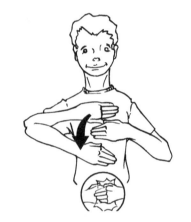  

Get   all   our   animals   ready

Here   comes the   circus   train

Copyright © 2011 Time to Sign, Inc.

Circus Train - cont.

All aboard the circus train

The circus train, the circus train

Line up for the circus train

Circus Train - cont.

The circus train (3X) (Chorus)

First car, pigs (sound 3X)

Second car, lions (sound 1X)

Ready, Set, Sign
Songs for Everyday Transitions

Circus Train - cont.

Third car, dogs (sound 4X)

Four car, elephants (sound 1X)

Fifth car, monkeys (sound 4X)

Copyright © 2011 Time to Sign, Inc.

10

Circus Train - cont.

Sixth car, horses (sound 1X)

Repeat Chorus

Ready, Set, Sign
Songs for Everyday Transitions

Copyright © 2011 Time to Sign, Inc.

Ready, Set, Sign
Songs for Everyday Transitions

Clean Up - Sign & Find

We are cleaning up

Sign then find (3X)

We are cleaning up

Copyright © 2011 Time to Sign, Inc.

Clean Up - Sign & Find - cont.

Sign then find (3X)

Pick up toys,   sign   toys,   find   toys

We are cleaning up

Pick up the blocks, sign blocks,   find   blocks

Ready, Set, Sign
Songs for Everyday Transitions

Clean Up - Sign & Find - cont.

We are cleaning up

Pick up the puzzles, sign puzzles, find puzzles

We are cleaning up

Pick up books, sign books, find books

Copyright © 2011 Time to Sign, Inc.

Clean Up - Sign & Find - cont.

We are cleaning up

Pick up the clothes, sign clothes, find clothes

We are cleaning up

Pick up crayons, sign crayons, find crayons

Ready, Set, Sign
Songs for Everyday Transitions

Clean Up - Sign & Find - cont.

We are cleaning up

Pick up the cars,   sign   cars,   find   cars

We are cleaning up

Pick up the dolls,   sign   dolls,   find   dolls

Copyright © 2011 Time to Sign, Inc.

16

Ready, Set, Sign
Songs for Everyday Transitions

Clean Up - Sign & Find - cont.

Repeat Chorus

Please put away   gently,   carefully, respectfully.

Please put away   gently,   carefully, respectfully.

Copyright © 2011 Time to Sign, Inc.

Ready, Set, Sign
Songs for Everyday Transitions

Color Fun

Stand up if you are wearing red

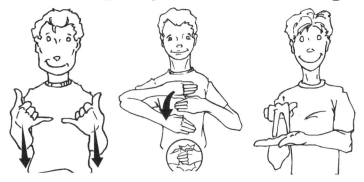

Now everybody stand up Turn (Repeat 12X)

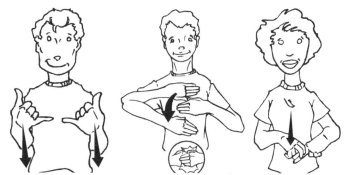

Now everybody sit down

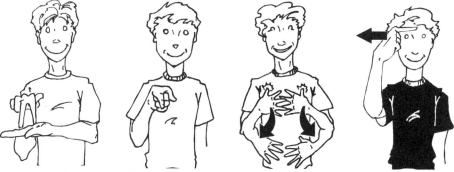

Stand up if you are wearing black

Copyright © 2011 Time to Sign, Inc.

Color Fun - cont.

Now   everybody   stand up

Hop (Repeat 12X)

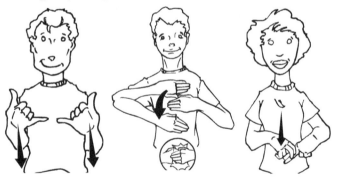
Now   everybody   sit down

Stand up if you are wearing   green

Ready, Set, Sign
Songs for Everyday Transitions

Color Fun - cont.

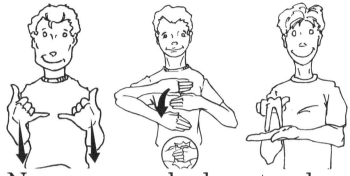

Now everybody stand up

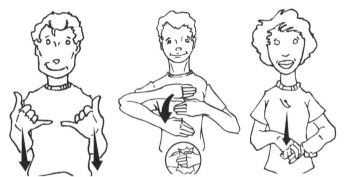

Shake (Repeat 12X) Now everybody sit down

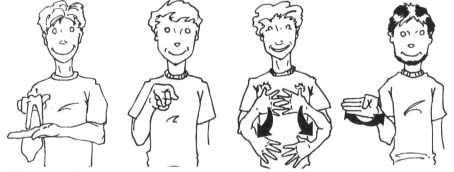

Stand up if you are wearing   blue

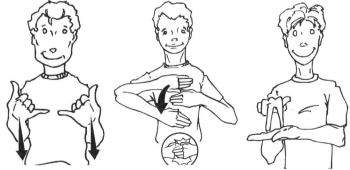

Now everybody stand up

Copyright © 2011 Time to Sign, Inc.

Color Fun - cont.

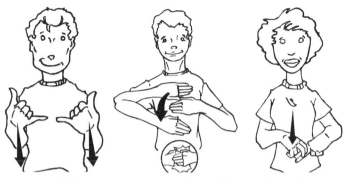

Clap (Repeat 12X)   Now everybody sit down

Stand up if you are wearing white

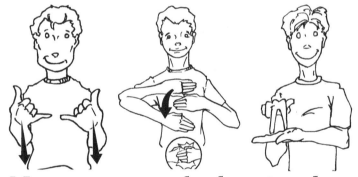

Now   everybody   stand up

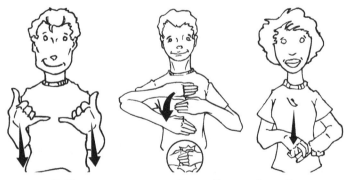

Jump (Repeat 12X)   Now everybody sit down

Color Fun - cont.

Stand up if you are wearing yellow

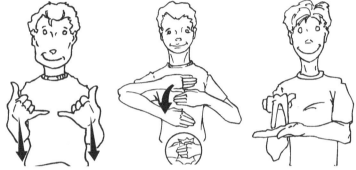

Now everybody stand up

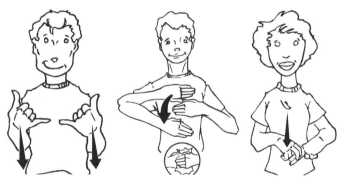

Snap (Repeat 12X)   Now everybody sit down

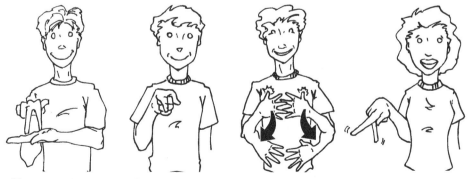

Stand up if you are wearing purple

Color Fun - cont.

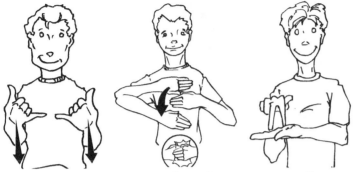

Now   everybody   stand up

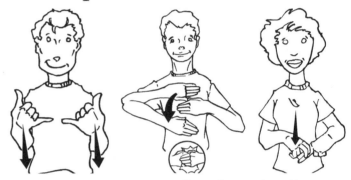

Stomp (Repeat 12X)   Now everybody sit down

Stand up if you are wearing   pink

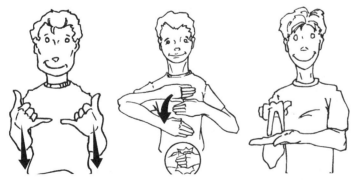

Now   everybody   stand up

Ready, Set, Sign
Songs for Everyday Transitions

Color Fun - cont.

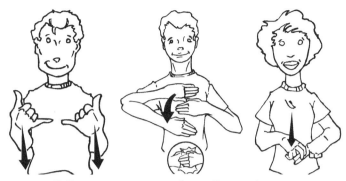

Reach (Repeat 12X)　　　Now everybody sit down

Copyright © 2011 Time to Sign, Inc.

24      Ready, Set, Sign
Songs for Everyday Transitions

Food Pyramid

Snack time, snack time

the food pyramid (Repeat 2X)

Snack time, snack time

healthy food today (Chorus).

Eating cereals, eating bread

Copyright © 2011 Time to Sign, Inc.

Ready, Set, Sign
Songs for Everyday Transitions

Food Pyramid - cont.

fruits and vegetables

like apples and carrots.

Drinking milk, eating chicken

Eating fish, lots of tasty meats.

No fats, no oils, or sweets.

Copyright © 2011 Time to Sign, Inc.

26

Ready, Set, Sign
Songs for Everyday Transitions

Food Pyramid - cont.

Chorus

Peanut butter and jelly too.

Yogurt and jello are good for you.

Fruits and vegetables like berries and corn.

Copyright © 2011 Time to Sign, Inc.

Food Pyramid - cont.

Lots of water and juice too.

Learning the food pyramid

is good for you.

Chorus

Goodbye Teachers & Friends

Teachers friends maestros amigos.

Teachers and friends, maestros y amigos

(Repeat 1X)

Good bye teachers and friends.

Copyright © 2011 Time to Sign, Inc.

Goodbye Teachers & Friends - cont.

Adios maestros y amigos (Chorus)

We learned A B C's.

Aprendimos A B C's

We learned 1 - 2 - 3's.

Goodbye Teachers & Friends - cont.

Aprendimos uno, dos, tres.

We had fun at school.

Nos divertimos en la escuela.

We had fun at school.

Goodbye Teachers & Friends - cont.

Nos divertimos en la escuela.

Chorus

Good Morning Teachers & Friends

Teachers friends maestros amigos.

Teachers and friends, maestros y amigos

(Repeat 1X)

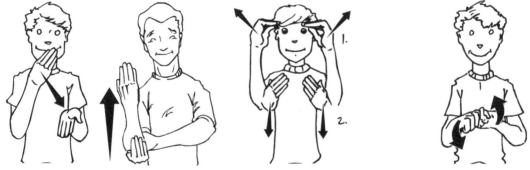

Good morning teachers and friends.

Good Morning Teachers & Friends - cont.

Good Morning Teachers & Friends - cont.

Aprender uno, dos, tres

Fun at school.

Divertirse en la escuela.

Fun at school.

Good Morning Teachers & Friends - cont.

Divertirse en la escuela.

Chorus

If You're Happy and You Know It

If you're happy and you know it, clap your hands (clap, clap). (Repeat 1X)

If you're happy and you know it,   your   face will surely show it.

If you're happy and you know it, clap your hands (clap, clap).

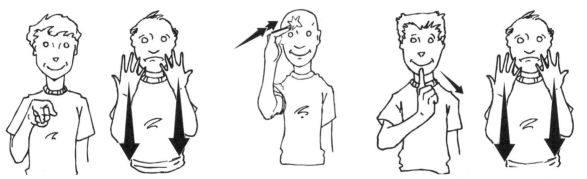

If you're   sad and you   know it, say, "boo, hoo." (Repeat 1X)

Copyright © 2011 Time to Sign, Inc.

Ready, Set, Sign
Songs for Everyday Transitions

If You're Happy and You Know It - cont.

If you're sad and you know it, your face will surely show it.

If you're sad and you know it, say, "boo, hoo."

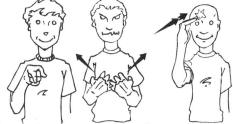

If you're angry and you know it, stomp your feet. (stomp) (Repeat 1X)

If you're angry and you know it, your face will surely show it.

If you're angry and you know it, stomp your feet. (stomp)

Copyright © 2011 Time to Sign, Inc.

If You're Happy and You Know It - cont.

If you're happy and you know it, clap your hands (clap, clap). (Repeat 1X)

If you're happy and you know it, then your   face will surely show it.

If you're happy and you know it, clap your hands (clap, clap).

March and Sing

Along the trail   we   march and sing,

march and sing, march and sing.

Along the trail   we   march and sing,

Along the trail   today.

March and Sing - cont.

Additional Versus:

We huff and puff (breathe heavily).

Swing our arms (swing arms at sides).

Ready, Set, Sign
Songs for Everyday Transitions

41

Mr. Sun

Oh Mister Sun, sun, Mister Golden Sun

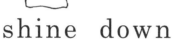

please   shine   down   on   me.

Oh Mister Sun, sun, Mister Golden Sun

hiding   behind   a   tree.

Copyright © 2011 Time to Sign, Inc.

Mr. Sun - cont.

These little children are asking you to please come out so

we can play with you.

Oh Mister Sun, sun, Mister Golden Sun

Ready, Set, Sign
Songs for Everyday Transitions

Mr. Sun - cont.

please shine down, please shine down

please   shine   down   on me.

Ready, Set, Sign
Songs for Everyday Transitions

Play Time

Play   time,

come on its play   time.

Play   time,

come   play   with   me.
(Repeat 1X) (Chorus)

Copyright © 2011 Time to Sign, Inc.

Play Time - cont.

O - U - T - S - I - D - E (Repeat 2X)

Outside time for you and me.

Let's run, let's climb,

Let's jump, let's dance.

Play Time - cont.

Let's run, let's climb,

Let's jump, let's dance.

Chorus (2X)

Feeling the sun

Ready, Set, Sign
Songs for Everyday Transitions  47

Play Time - cont.

Swinging on swings

Digging the sand

Making some friends

Feeling the sun

Copyright © 2011 Time to Sign, Inc.

Play Time - cont.

Swinging on swings

Digging the sand

Making some friends

Chorus (2X)

Rest Time

I　　want　you to lie down

Children follow song instructions:

Slowly close your eyes

Put your hands at your side

Take a deep breath in

Let it out

Now listen to the music

And relax

School Bus

The school bus comes for me. (Repeat)

Hey, ho, its time to go.

The school bus comes for me.

First we pick up (use letter of name or sign name).

School Bus - cont.

Next   we   pick up   (use letter of name or sign name).

Then   we   pick up   (use letter of name or sign name).

(Repeat for all members of the class.)

Last   we   pick up   (use letter of name or sign name).

School Bus - cont.

Now   we're   all at school. (Repeat 1X)

Clap and cheer   we're finally here.

Now   we're   all at school.

Ready, Set, Sign
Songs for Everyday Transitions

Traffic Light

Can you see the traffic light,

the traffic light, the traffic light?

Green means go and yellow means slow,

Copyright © 2011 Time to Sign, Inc.

Traffic Light - cont.

and red means STOP, STOP, STOP!

(Repeat song)

Ready, Set, Sign
Songs for Everyday Transitions    55

Twinkle Twinkle Little Star

Twinkle,   twinkle,   little   star,

how   I   wonder   what   you are.

Up   above   the   world   so   high,

Copyright © 2011 Time to Sign, Inc.

Twinkle Twinkle Little Star - cont.

like   a   diamond in the sky.

Twinkle,   twinkle,   little   star,

how   I   wonder what you are.

Copyright © 2011 Time to Sign, Inc.

Ready, Set, Sign
Songs for Everyday Transitions

Wake Up

Boys and girls let's wake up,

waking up, waking up. (Repeat 1X) (Chorus)

Body movement to music...
Now clap, clap, clap your hands
Right hand up, now shake shake
Left hand up, shake shake
Both hands up, shake shake
Hands on your head, shake shake
Hands on your shoulders, shake shake
Hands on your hips, now shake shake
Hand on your knees, shake shake
Now touch your toes, shake shake
Lift straight up, shake shake
Chorus (Repeat 1X)

Copyright © 2011 Time to Sign, Inc.

Wake Up - cont.

Right foot out, stomp stomp

Left foot out, stomp stomp

Both feet out, stomp stomp

Hands on your hips, stomp stomp

Hands on your shoulders, stomp stomp

Hands on your head, stomp stomp

Both hands out, stomp stomp

Chorus (Repeat 1X)

Now we are all up, let's go.

Ready, Set, Sign
Songs for Everyday Transitions

What Are We Doing Today

What are we   doing   today? (Repeat 1X)

Look at the clock,   look at the time.

What are we   doing   today? (Chorus)

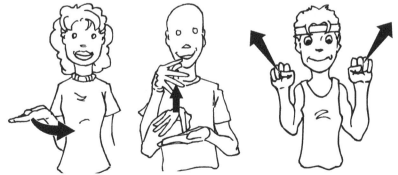

Welcome, snack, exercise,

Copyright © 2011 Time to Sign, Inc.

What Are We Doing Today - cont.

circle   time,   A   B   C's.

Chorus

Music,   arts,   reading too,

puzzle time, story   time, math.

What Are We Doing Today - cont.

Chorus

Play, drama, nap time too,

Science, potty, going home.

Chorus

Classroom Management Phrases

sit in a circle/sentarse

story time/leer un cuento

pay attention/atento

stop now/pare ahora

find a seat/encontrar un asiento

let's clean it up/vamos a limpiar

nap time/siesta

close your eyes/cierra los ojos

Copyright © 2011 Time to Sign, Inc.

Ready, Set, Sign
Songs for Everyday Transitions

Classroom Management Phrases - cont.

go to cubbie/ir a tu cubbie

put away/ubicar

play time/tiempo de jugar

potty time/ir al baño

snack time/ merienda

I'm hungry/ Tengo hambre

pick me up/ recogerme

going home/ir a casa

Copyright © 2011 Time to Sign, Inc.

Classroom Management Signs

bring - llevar

dance - bailar

do - hacer

line up
- ponerse en fila

play - jugar

potty - baño

sit - sentarse

stand up
- ponerse de pie

Copyright © 2011 Time to Sign, Inc.

Ready, Set, Sign
Songs for Everyday Transitions

65

Classroom Management Signs - cont.

listen - escuchar

now - ahora

sleep - dormir

quiet - silencio

eat - comer

voice - voz

outside - fuera

inside - dentro

Copyright © 2011 Time to Sign, Inc.

Classroom Management Signs - cont.

Ready, Set, Sign
Songs for Everyday Transitions

Colors

colores - colors

rojo - red

azul - blue

verde - green

amarillo - yellow

blanco - white

negro - black

café - brown

Copyright © 2011 Time to Sign, Inc.

Emotions

 afraid - temeroso

 angry - enojado

 excited - entusiasmado

 happy - alegre

 love - amor

 sad - triste

 silly - tonto

 tired - cansado

Ready, Set, Sign
Songs for Everyday Transitions

69

Family & Greetings

father - padre

mother - madre

grandfather - abuelo

grandmother - abuela

hello - hola

goodbye - adiós

good morning - buenos dias

good night - buenas noches

Copyright © 2011 Time to Sign, Inc.

Ready, Set, Sign
Songs for Everyday Transitions

Manners

manners - modales

please - por favor

thank you - gracias

you're welcome - de nada

yes - sí

no - no

excuse me - perdón

may I? - puedo yo/mi?

Copyright © 2011 Time to Sign, Inc.

Ready, Set, Sign
Songs for Everyday Transitions      71

Numbers

  uno - one - 1   dos - two - 2

  tres - three - 3   cuatro - four - 4

  cinco - five - 5   seis - six - 6

  siete - seven - 7   ocho - eight - 8

  nueve - nine - 9   diez - ten - 10

Copyright © 2011 Time to Sign, Inc.

Snacks

snacks - bocado

cookie - galleta

crackers - galleta

fruit - frutas

grapes - uvas

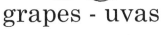
juice - jugo

apple - manzana

vegetables - vegetales

Ready, Set, Sign
Songs for Everyday Transitions

Transportation

car - carro

boat - bote

bicycle - bicicleta

truck - camión

train - tren

helicopter - helicóptero

bus - autobus

airplane - aeroplano

Copyright © 2011 Time to Sign, Inc.

Ready, Set, Sign
Songs for Everyday Transitions

Classroom Materials

Time to Sign Pledge of Allegiance Poster
This 18" x 24" poster teaches children the nation's pledge in easy-to-follow sign!

Our classroom materials help teach students and encourage further learning.

Time to Sign Alphabet Wall Chart
Post this ASL alphabet on your wall to support children's learning. Features upper and lower case letters, the handshape for each letter, and a description of how to sign an example word.

Time to Sign Placemats
This set of 4 double-sided placemats feature the alphabet, animals, colors, family, numbers, school, and seasons signs. Placemats are treated with durable 5 mil thick, easy-to-clean plastic for use in eating and arts areas, or for posting on walls or glass. Over 120 signs in all!

Time to Sign Infants Small Placemat
This placemat features 18 common infant signs, such as mother, father, yes, no, please, thank you, bath, love, and milk. Placemats are treated with durable 5 mil thick, easy-to-clean plastic for use in eating and arts areas, or for posting on walls or glass.

PO Box 33831
Indialantic, FL 32903
Phone (321) 726-9466
www.timetosign.com
contact@timetosign.com

Contact us at 321.259.0976 or contact@timetosign.com for more information!

Copyright © 2011 Time to Sign, Inc.

Ready, Set, Sign
Songs for Everyday Transitions

Our Original Learning Books

Time to Sign with Children Learning Guide

The Learning Guide is a great beginner book for teachers and parents. It covers how to incorporate sign language into your daily routine. Includes Developmental communication milestones and age-appropriate signs and activities from birth to five years. Features over 200 sign illustrations, including the alphabet, animals, emotions, family signs, manners, food, and much more. The book also now comes with DVD demonstrations of all signs in book!

The original Time to Sign Learning Books Series covers all ages of children, from infant to school-age, and all feature English, Spanish, and Sign.

Time to Sign Preschool Sign Language Book

This book has over 300 sign illustrations that are specific to the preschool learning environment. Children learn how to use American Sign Language (ASL) to communicate: manners, emotions, family, colors, transportation, opposites, and much more. Teachers learn signs for classroom managment.

Time to Sign School Age Sign Language Book

This book contains nearly 1000 sign illustrations for school age children. With age-appropriate signs to include such areas as: Occupations, insects, pronouns, questions, seasons, sports, math, science, common signs and phrases, and much more.

Time to Sign, Inc.
PO Box 33831
Indialantic, FL 32903
Phone (321) 726-9466
www.timetosign.com
contact@timetosign.com

Contact us at 321.259.0976 or contact@timetosign.com for more information!

Copyright © 2011 Time to Sign, Inc.

Time to Sign with Children DVD

10 topical signing areas, 17 songs, and 3 stories

Our most popular DVD, children learn to sign the fun way with Time to Sign founder Lillian Hubler and friends in this 53-minute video your children will want to watch over and over again!

Topics include the alphabet, numbers, greetings, family, manners, colors, animals, food, and utensils, as well as a section just for parents and teachers, Benefits of Signing with Children.

Songs include the ABCs Song; BINGO; Hands Can Count; Six Little Ducks; Three Little Monkeys; Please & Thank You; Apples & Bananas; Muffin Man; Itsy Bitsy Spider; Row, Row, Row Your Boat; Twinkle, Twinkle Little Star; Where is Thumbkin?; If You're Happy & You Know It; and many more!

Stories include Tea Please; Peek-A-Boo Pets; The Colorful Tiger

Perfect for educators of young children to learn and teach American Sign Language (ASL) in the classroom!

PO Box 33831
Indialantic, FL 32903
Phone (321) 726-9466
www.timetosign.com
contact@timetosign.com

Contact us at 321.259.0976 or contact@timetosign.com for more information!

Copyright © 2011 Time to Sign, Inc.

Made in the USA
Middletown, DE
27 July 2019